One Picture

| 1 | one | • |

Look at the house.

One house.

1 house

Look at the sun.

One sun.

1 sun

Look at the cloud.

One cloud.

1 cloud

Look at the tree.

One tree.

1 tree

Look at the bird.

One bird.

1 bird

Look at the cat.

One cat.

1 cat

Look at the dog.

One dog.

1 dog

one cloud

one sun

one house

one bird

one dog

one cat

one tree

one picture